All rights reserved. Printed in the UK. No part of this book may be used or reproduced in any manner whatsoever without written permission except in the case of brief quotations embodied in critical articles or reviews.

First published in 2024 by PRESS DIONYSUS LTD in the UK, 167, Portland Road, N15 4SZ, London.

By Pearl Zander

Book cover & interior layout design: Semiha Deniz Akıncı

ISBN: 978-1-913961-43-5

Copyright © 2024 by PRESS DIONYSUS.

· e-mail: info@pressdionysus.com

· web: www.pressdionysus.com

Stray Kids, the vibrant K-pop sensation that made waves in 2017, has captured hearts all around the globe, all thanks to the delightful whirlwind that is JYP Entertainment's reality show, *Stray Kids*. From day one, they've danced to the beat of their own drum, crafting their own songs and weaving messages that resonate with the youthful spirit everywhere. Originally a lively gang of nine, they've evolved into a formidable team of eight, featuring the charismatic Bang Chan (the fearless leader), along with the dynamic Lee Know, Changbin, Hyunjin, Han, Felix, Seungmin, and the ever-charming I.N.

So, what's the secret sauce that makes Stray Kids shine like a disco ball in a dark room? It's their extraordinary knack for blending genres! Picture this: a high-octane mix of hip-hop, EDM, and rock, all swirled together to create tracks that are bursting with energy and ready to get everyone on their feet. It's a sound that not only pumps up your adrenaline but also brings a smile to your face. Talk about a soundtrack for living life to the fullest!

But it's not just the music that makes them stand out; it's their message! They tackle themes of self-discovery, resilience, and authenticity, reminding us all to embrace our true selves. Each performance is not just a display of talent; it's a celebration of individuality and connection. So, whether you're dancing in your room or bopping along on the bus, Stray Kids invites you to join the party! Grab your friends and turn up the volume—life's too short not to have a little fun!

Stray Kids are far more than your average K-pop group—they're a powerhouse of creativity and passion! With members like Bang Chan, Changbin, and Han (collectively known as 3RACHA) steering much of their music and production, you can really feel the dedication they put into every single track. Their hard work has certainly paid off, as STAYs (their devoted fans) can't get enough of the electrifying performances and relatable lyrics that showcase their incredible charisma!

With hit albums like *GO LIVE*, *IN LIFE*, and *NOEASY,* Stray Kids have truly made their mark on the global music scene. But they don't just stop at creating music; they're always on the move, touring the world and connecting with fans in every corner. It's this unwavering connection, along with their emotionally charged, self-produced sound, that sets them apart as a truly unique force in K-pop.

What really makes Stray Kids shine is their boldness and authenticity. They consistently push boundaries while smashing records, showing everyone that they're not just another K-pop group—they're a global phenomenon! So, let's keep cheering them on as they continue to inspire and captivate us all with their artistry and energy!

Bang Chan

- **Real Name:** Bahng Christopher Chahn
- **Stage Name:** Bang Chan
- **Position:** Leader, Lead Vocalist, Lead Dancer, Producer
- **Birthday:** October 3, 1997
- **Zodiac Sign:** Libra
- **Blood Type:** O
- **Place of Birth:** Seoul, South Korea (but moved to Sydney, Australia, at a young age)
- **Height:** 171 cm (5'7")
- **Weight:** 65 kg (143 lbs)
- **Family:** Father, mother, younger sister, younger brother
- **Favourite Colour:** Black
- **Hobbies:** Producing music, working out, hanging out with friends
- **Lucky Number:** 3
- **Fun Fact:** He trained for 7 years before debuting and is fluent in English (he grew up in Australia).
- **Guilty Pleasures:** Watching K-dramas (he enjoys binge-watching when he has free time) and late-night snacks like ramen.

Bang Chan, whose full name is Bahng Christopher Chahn, was born on October 3, 1997, in Seoul, South Korea, but he spent his formative years in Sydney, Australia—what a delightful blend of cultures! Fans and friends affectionately call him "Chan," and he's lovingly referred to as "The Leader" for his incredible role in Stray Kids. He truly embodies charisma and creativity!

He's incredibly multilingual, speaking Korean, English, and even a bit of Japanese! His English fluency blossomed during his time in Australia, where he immersed himself in the language and culture. From a young age, he was passionate about music, shining in school plays and talent shows. These experiences ignited his dream of making it in the entertainment industry! When it comes to food, Bang Chan has a zest for life! He adores Korean barbecue and sushi but is always excited to explore new dishes from around the globe.

In his downtime, you'll catch him immersing himself in video games, rocking out to his favourite tunes, or snuggling with his beloved pets. He's also dedicated to staying active, regularly hitting the gym to ensure he's in top shape for those fantastic performances. And when he's in the mood, he loves to experiment with new recipes in the kitchen! These passions make him incredibly relatable and down-to-earth, earning him the affection of fans everywhere!

What makes Bang Chan truly special is his playful and cheeky side, especially when it comes to gaming! He loves sharing hilarious tales about his video game adventures with friends and fellow members, showcasing his competitive spirit and infectious sense of humour. Whether he's teasing others or pulling light-hearted pranks, his fun-loving nature adds so much joy to the group and brings smiles all around!

Bang Chan isn't just an incredible musician; he's a fantastic leader too! Like the big brother of the group, he always supports his teammates and encourages their growth. His warm and caring nature has truly resonated with fans and members alike, proving that he's not just about the music—he's also a genuinely fun-loving person!

Bang Chan, the charismatic leader of Stray Kids, is not just a musical genius; he's incredibly relatable and down-to-earth! His passion for music production really shines as he shares behind-the-scenes glimpses with fans—whether it's crafting heartfelt lyrics or creating catchy beats. By bringing fans along on his creative journey, he shows that anyone can chase their dreams! His inspiring journey from Australia to the K-pop stage proves that hard work truly pays off. With personal stories of struggle and perseverance, Bang Chan encourages fans to believe in themselves and keep pushing through tough times. What a remarkable role model!

Bang Chan is an absolute trendsetter with his unique fusion of streetwear and edgy styles! His outfits perfectly reflect his vibrant personality and creativity, solidifying his status as a style icon for teens. By daring to experiment with different looks, he encourages fans to embrace their individuality and express themselves through fashion. How inspiring is that!

Bang Chan genuinely cares for his fans, and it shows in every heartfelt message and fan event he's part of. He has a knack for making each STAY feel special, connecting with them directly through social media and lively Q&As. His love for his fans truly shines in all that he does!

With his charismatic personality, incredible creativity, and deep passion for music, Bang Chan isn't just a leader; he's a true role model for all of us! He shows how hard work and determination can turn our dreams into reality. What an inspiration!

Lee Know

- **Real Name:** Lee Minho
- **Stage Name:** Lee Know
- **Position:** Main Dancer, Vocalist, Rapper
- **Birthday:** October 25, 1998
- **Zodiac Sign:** Scorpio
- **Blood Type:** O
- **Place of Birth:** Gimpo, South Korea
- **Height:** 172 cm (5'8")
- **Weight:** 64 kg (141 lbs)
- **Favourite Colour:** Mint
- **Hobbies:** Watching movies, choreographing dances, playing with his three cats
- **Lucky Number:** 7
- **Fun Fact:** Lee Know is known for his exceptional dance skills and was a backup dancer for BTS before debuting with Stray Kids.
- **Guilty Pleasures:** Cat videos (he's obsessed with cats and can watch videos of them for hours) and junk food like chips.

Lee Know, born Lee Minho on 25th October 1998 in Gimpo, South Korea, has always dazzled with his incredible dance moves! Fans absolutely adore his playful, cheeky nature, especially during gaming sessions and light-hearted teasing with the other members—he truly brings a joyful, unpredictable energy to everything! Plus, his remarkable ability to use both hands equally well makes him a standout talent!

Affectionately known as "Minho" by friends and fans, he's incredibly versatile! Fluent in Korean and well-versed in Japanese and English, he shines on the global stage. A true foodie at heart, he adores spicy dishes and Korean BBQ—just like Bang Chan! But he's always up for an adventure, ready to try something new. What a delight!

Beyond his incredible dance skills, Lee Know showcases an artistic flair with his passion for photography, capturing stunning aesthetic shots. He's also a dedicated animal lover, with a soft spot for his three adorable cats. While he may not be super active on personal social media, his vibrant presence in Stray Kids' content always shines through!

Before joining Stray Kids, Lee Know worked as a backup dancer for various K-pop artists, making his journey to idol status truly inspiring. He exemplifies how hard work and persistence can turn dreams into reality! While he appears fearless on stage, he actually has a fear of heights. Yet, during the Stray Kids challenges, he bravely faced this fear, showcasing his incredible determination! What a fantastic role model!

Lee Know's style is effortlessly cool and minimal, yet he spices things up with bold accessories and one-of-a-kind jackets! As a true trendsetter, he inspires his fans to embrace their own unique style with confidence. How fabulous is that?

Lee Know's personality is absolutely captivating! He seamlessly oscillates between playful mischief and deep contemplation. His love for animals and genuine caring nature make him so relatable. Plus, his attention to detail in dance and interactions really shines through, blending fun with heartfelt moments that leave a lasting impression. A popular inside joke among STAYs is his cheeky tendency to mysteriously disappear during live streams, sparking curiosity about whether he's off enjoying time with his cats or concocting his next playful prank! Isn't he just delightful?

Lee Know has big dreams of choreographing dance routines, not just for Stray Kids but for other artists too! With his incredible eye for detail and genuine passion for dance, this goal feels completely within reach. We are eagerly looking forward to witnessing his exciting journey ahead!

Changbin

- **Real Name:** Seo Changbin
- **Stage Name:** Changbin
- **Position:** Main Rapper, Vocalist, Producer
- **Birthday:** August 11, 1999
- **Zodiac Sign:** Leo
- **Blood Type:** O
- **Place of Birth:** Yongin, South Korea
- **Height:** 167 cm (5'6")
- **Weight:** 68 kg (150 lbs)
- **Family:** Father, mother, elder sister
- **Favourite Colour:** Black
- **Hobbies:** Shopping for clothes, listening to music
- **Lucky Number:** 4
- **Fun Fact:** Changbin is part of Stray Kids' production team, 3RACHA, and is recognized for his fast rap style.
- **Guilty Pleasures:** Working out late at night (he loves fitness and might push himself too much) and indulging in sweet treats like chocolate.

Changbin, whose full name is Seo Chang-bin, was born on 11th August 1999 in Seongbuk-dong, Seoul, South Korea. From an early age, he developed a deep passion for music, particularly rap. His playful nature truly comes alive during games and challenges, showcasing his wonderfully competitive spirit. Affectionately known as "Binnie," he brings joy and energy to every gathering, earning the endearing nickname "Silly Binnie" from fans who can't get enough of his delightful antics!

Changbin is a language lover who speaks fluent Korean and is eagerly improving his English to connect with fans worldwide! His passion for spicy dishes like tteokbokki is infectious, and he thrives on exploring new flavours from different cultures. Not only is he an incredible rapper with a distinctive deep voice, but he's also a talented producer and songwriter, playing a vital role in shaping Stray Kids' music. His creativity and enthusiasm truly shine through in everything he does!

In his downtime, you'll often find him diving into video games or working out at the gym, sharing his fitness journey with fans who admire his commitment. A vibrant presence on social media, especially Instagram, he connects with followers by giving them a sneak peek into his life. With his remarkable talent and approachable personality, Changbin shines as a relatable and inspiring member of Stray Kids, reminding everyone that a blend of passion and fun can lead to amazing achievements!

Changbin's journey to joining Stray Kids was filled with challenges, but he persevered with incredible determination! After three rigorous years of training at JYP Entertainment, he sometimes grappled with self-doubt. Instead of giving up, he leaned on his friends and fellow trainees for support, bravely pushing through tough times. His debut with Stray Kids is a shining testament to the power of hard work, inspiring fans everywhere to believe in themselves and tackle their own challenges. What a fantastic journey!

Changbin's aspirations are truly inspiring! He's eager to grow as an artist and collaborate with a diverse range of musicians, spanning hip-hop, rock, and everything in between. With a passion for music production, he aims to create songs that resonate with everyone, no matter their background. Exciting times ahead!

Hyunjin

- **Real Name:** Hwang Hyunjin
- **Stage Name:** Hyunjin
- **Position:** Main Dancer, Lead Rapper, Visual
- **Birthday:** March 20, 2000
- **Zodiac Sign:** Pisces
- **Blood Type:** B
- **Place of Birth:** Seoul, South Korea
- **Height:** 179 cm (5'10.5")
- **Weight:** 61 kg (134 lbs)
- **Family:** Father, mother, only child
- **Favourite Colour:** Black and white
- **Hobbies:** Dancing, drawing, playing with his dog, Kkami
- **Lucky Number:** 1
- **Fun Fact:** Hyunjin is known for his charismatic stage presence and is one of the most popular members globally.
- **Guilty Pleasures:** Buying too many art supplies (he enjoys painting) and playing video games late into the night.

Hyunjin, whose full name is Hwang Hyun-jin, was born on March 20, 2000, in Seoul, South Korea. From an early age, he was completely enchanted by dance and the arts! His remarkable talent has earned him countless trophies in dance competitions, fuelling his passion for performance. With a lively spirit that brightens any space, he has a unique ability to make everyone laugh out loud. His friends love to tease him about his over-the-top reactions when he faces defeat in games, creating unforgettable, hilarious moments that fans absolutely cherish!

Affectionately called "Jinnie" by friends and fans alike, he's all about building connections—learning English to engage with fans across the globe. A true foodie at heart, he enjoys everything from sashimi to pizza and kimchi! His culinary adventures are always a delight, and he loves sharing these exciting experiences with everyone.

Hyunjin isn't just an incredible dancer; he's also a talented artist! He loves expressing himself through drawing and often shares his artwork with fans, showcasing his creative flair. When he's not performing, you might catch him enjoying video games, binge-watching films, or sharing delightful snippets of his life on social media!

Speaking of social media, Hyunjin is a total pro! He brings joy and positivity to his Instagram posts, effortlessly connecting with fans. It's as if he invites everyone to join him on his journey, making each follower feel special and included.

Hyunjin's journey to joining Stray Kids was anything but easy! After years of training at JYP Entertainment, he encountered numerous challenges along the way. Yet, rather than surrendering, he turned those hurdles into a source of strength and resilience. His inspiring story encourages fans to persevere, proving that hard work truly pays off, no matter the obstacles!

Hyunjin is an absolute fashion icon! He loves to experiment with various looks, brilliantly showcasing his bold, creative, and playful personality through his outfits. He never fails to turn heads and make a remarkable statement!

And let's not forget how he loves to steal the spotlight during performances! With his mesmerizing presence and stunning visuals, it's hard to take your eyes off him when he's on stage—his energy is truly magnetic!

Hyunjin has sky-high dreams! He's dedicated to evolving as an artist and crafting unforgettable moments for us. The idea of collaborating with musicians from different genres fills him with excitement! His ambition and passion truly inspire everyone around him.

Han

- **Real Name:** Han Jisung
- **Stage Name:** Han
- **Position:** Main Rapper, Lead Vocalist, Producer
- **Birthday:** September 14, 2000
- **Zodiac Sign:** Virgo
- **Blood Type:** B
- **Place of Birth:** Incheon, South Korea
- **Height:** 169 cm (5'7")
- **Weight:** 62 kg (137 lbs)
- **Family:** Father, mother, elder brother
- **Favourite Colour:** Red
- **Hobbies:** Watching movies, eating cheesecake, playing video games
- **Lucky Number:** 5
- **Fun Fact:** Han is also part of the 3RACHA team and is known for his versatility in both singing and rapping.
- **Guilty Pleasures:** Reading webtoons or comics for hours and late-night snacks like fried chicken.

Han, whose real name is Han Jisung, was born on 14th September 2000 in Incheon, South Korea. His passion for music and performing has always shone brightly. Prior to joining Stray Kids, he lived in Malaysia for a few years, where he not only picked up English but also broadened his worldview. These rich experiences make him a relatable and cherished figure among fans across the globe!

Affectionately nicknamed "Squirrel" by friends and fans alike, Han is the vibrant spirit of Stray Kids! With his lively, energetic moves and cheeky personality, he never fails to lighten the mood. Whether he's cracking jokes, playfully teasing his bandmates, or goofing around during games, Han's infectious enthusiasm keeps everyone smiling. His fun-loving nature truly brings the group to life!

Han's fluency in both Korean and English allows him to bond effortlessly with fans globally. And let's not forget his sweet tooth! He has a particular fondness for cheesecake, chocolate cake, and just about anything deliciously sugary. Fans absolutely love hearing him share his snack favourites during interviews—it's such a delightful glimpse into his personality!

Han isn't just a skilled rapper; he's also an incredible singer and songwriter! He plays a vital role in Stray Kids' music, infusing his own lyrics and melodies into their tracks. His deep, soulful voice brings a distinct flair to their sound, and his creative spirit shines brightly in each song. When he's not in the studio, you can find him unwinding by writing lyrics, watching movies, or enjoying video games. How cool is that?

Though he may not post as often as some of the other members, when Han does share on social media, it's always a beautiful and meaningful moment! His posts offer fans a lovely glimpse into his personal thoughts and daily life, making them feel even more connected to him. It's always a treat to see what he shares!

Han's fashion sense is the perfect blend of laid-back and stylish! He of edge, whether he's sporting a hoodie or experimenting with bold accessories. His look always exudes a cool vibe that truly reflects his vibrant personality. Love it!

Fun facts about Han reveal his delightful quirks! He has this charming habit of talking to himself when he's nervous or deep in thought, and his bandmates love to tease him about it. Plus, there's a long-standing inside joke about his impeccable timing for delivering laughter with his unexpected humour. Fans absolutely adore this playful yet introspective side of him, making him all the more relatable and lovable!

Han is incredibly passionate about his growth as an artist, both with Stray Kids and as a soloist! He's consistently exploring fresh ways to express himself musically, aiming to craft songs that truly resonate with people. His unwavering dedication and ambition are nothing short of inspiring, encouraging us to chase their dreams despite any challenges they may encounter.

Felix

- **Real Name:** Lee Felix
- **Stage Name:** Felix
- **Position:** Lead Dancer, Lead Rapper
- **Birthday:** September 15, 2000
- **Zodiac Sign:** Virgo
- **Blood Type:** AB
- **Place of Birth:** Sydney, Australia
- **Height:** 171 cm (5'7")
- **Weight:** 64 kg (141 lbs)
- **Family:** Father, mother, elder sister, younger sister
- **Favourite Colour:** Black
- **Hobbies:** Playing video games, shopping, listening to music
- **Lucky Number:** 8
- **Fun Fact:** Felix is Australian and has a deep voice that contrasts with his bright, youthful appearance.
- **Guilty Pleasures:** Baking cookies (he's a talented baker) and sneaking in midnight snacks like ice cream.

Felix, whose full name is Lee Felix, brightened the world on September 15, 2000, in Sydney, Australia. Growing up in a vibrant, multicultural setting, he discovered his passion for music and dance at an early age. His spirited childhood nurtured his sense of adventure and open-mindedness. With a dream to join Stray Kids, Felix eagerly pursued his passion for performance, aiming to connect with fans through the enchanting world of music. What a journey!

Affectionately known as "Bunny" by friends and fans, Felix infuses Stray Kids with his vibrant, playful spirit. His infectious charm lights up any room, and he has an uncanny knack for cracking jokes that send everyone into fits of laughter. Whether he's in the midst of a game or just enjoying casual downtime, his cheeky side comes to life as he playfully teases his fellow members, ensuring every moment is filled with fun!

Fluent in both English and Korean, Felix effortlessly connects with fans worldwide. A true foodie at heart, he simply can't resist indulging in Korean fried chicken and pasta! His sweet tooth craves delightful treats like macarons and rice cakes. With a passion for culinary exploration, Felix loves sharing his delicious adventures, inviting fans to join him on a flavourful journey!

As a versatile performer, Felix isn't just an amazing dancer; he's also a captivating vocalist. His unique flair enhances Stray Kids' music, making their performances even more electrifying. Fans adore his deep voice and magnetic charisma, which truly set him apart. When he's not dazzling us on stage, you can catch Felix enjoying video games, binge-watching movies, or sharing fun moments on social media. He's a true gem!

Felix absolutely adores connecting with his fans on Instagram, sharing genuine snippets of his life that radiate warmth and positivity. His posts really make fans feel like they're part of his exciting journey!

When it comes to fashion, Felix's sense is as vibrant as his personality—he loves to blend casual and trendy styles, often showcasing bright colours and fun accessories. Whether he's lounging in a cosy hoodie or stepping out in something chic, he always exudes an effortlessly cool vibe!

Fun fact: Felix has a fantastic talent for mimicking his fellow group members, creating hilariously memorable moments and inside jokes that uplift everyone's spirits! A true animal lover at heart, he frequently shares delightful stories about his pets, which fans absolutely adore. His cheerful personality perfectly balances his more serious side, making him wonderfully relatable to everyone!

Felix is on an exciting journey to grow as an artist and inspire others through his music! He dreams of collaborating with a diverse range of musicians and diving into various genres, all while showcasing his creativity and passion. His unwavering determination and hard work motivate us to chase our dreams, reminding everyone that with heartfelt perseverance, anything is possible!

Seungmin

- **Real Name:** Kim Seungmin
- **Stage Name:** Seungmin
- **Position:** Lead Vocalist
- **Birthday:** September 22, 2000
- **Zodiac Sign:** Virgo
- **Blood Type:** A
- **Place of Birth:** Seoul, South Korea
- **Height:** 178 cm (5'10")
- **Weight:** 64 kg (141 lbs)
- **Family:** Father, mother, elder sister
- **Favourite Colour:** Purple
- **Hobbies:** Taking pictures, journaling
- **Lucky Number:** 9
- **Fun Fact:** Seungmin is known for his soothing voice and is considered the mood-maker of the group.
- **Guilty Pleasures:** Listening to soft ballads on repeat and indulging in comfort foods like instant noodles.

Seungmin, known as Kim Seungmin, was born on 22nd September 2000 in the vibrant city of Seoul, South Korea. From a young age, he was captivated by singing, eagerly participating in school plays and local talent shows, where he truly lit up the stage. His passion for music led him to a music academy, where he dedicated himself to honing his vocal skills and pursuing his dream of becoming an artist. These formative years set the stage for his incredible journey with Stray Kids, where he now stands out as a remarkable vocalist!

Seungmin is like the group's warm hug, naturally stepping into the "dad" role and looking out for his fellow members. He always knows just how to lift someone's spirits or offer a friendly ear, making him incredibly relatable to fans who cherish his genuine kindness. But don't be fooled—he's got a cheeky side too! During game nights, his competitive nature shines, and his playful jokes bring endless laughter, creating unforgettable memories for everyone.

Fluent in both Korean and English, Seungmin effortlessly connects with fans worldwide, making them feel right at home in his world. He has a particular fondness for eggs, enjoying them in every imaginable dish! And let's not forget his sweet tooth—he's especially passionate about chocolatey desserts. His adventurous spirit shines through as he eagerly explores new culinary delights, sharing every tasty experience with his fans along the way!

As a member of Stray Kids, Seungmin isn't just a brilliant singer; he infuses emotional depth into the group's music that resonates with fans. His voice adds a heartfelt touch that truly captivates. Off the stage, you'll often find him enjoying video games, binge-watching films, or simply hanging out with the other members. It's the perfect way for him to unwind and recharge!

Seungmin absolutely adores connecting with fans on social media, especially Instagram! His posts are brimming with delightful moments from his life, perfectly capturing his cheerful and playful personality. It's as if he's inviting fans to join him on his everyday adventures, creating a sense of closeness that's simply heartwarming!

Seungmin's fashion sense is a delightful blend of laid-back charm and chic elegance! He masterfully mixes comfortable pieces with trendy accents, often elevating his looks with eye-catching accessories that reflect his creative spirit. Whether he's rocking a classic t-shirt or a sharp jacket, he always exudes an effortlessly polished vibe. It's all about that easy style!

Seungmin is full of fun surprises! His knack for imitating various accents often sparks hilarious inside jokes with the group, keeping everyone entertained. He's also a passionate animal lover, especially when it comes to dogs, and shares heartwarming moments with his pets on social media that fans simply adore. His mix of humour and genuine warmth makes him an endearing figure that everyone can't help but love!

Seungmin's greatest dream is to continually evolve as an artist, creating music that genuinely touches hearts. He's excited to explore various genres and collaborate with diverse artists, showcasing his versatility and creative flair. His unwavering dedication and hard work motivate us all to chase our dreams and embrace our true selves. What an incredible journey he's on!

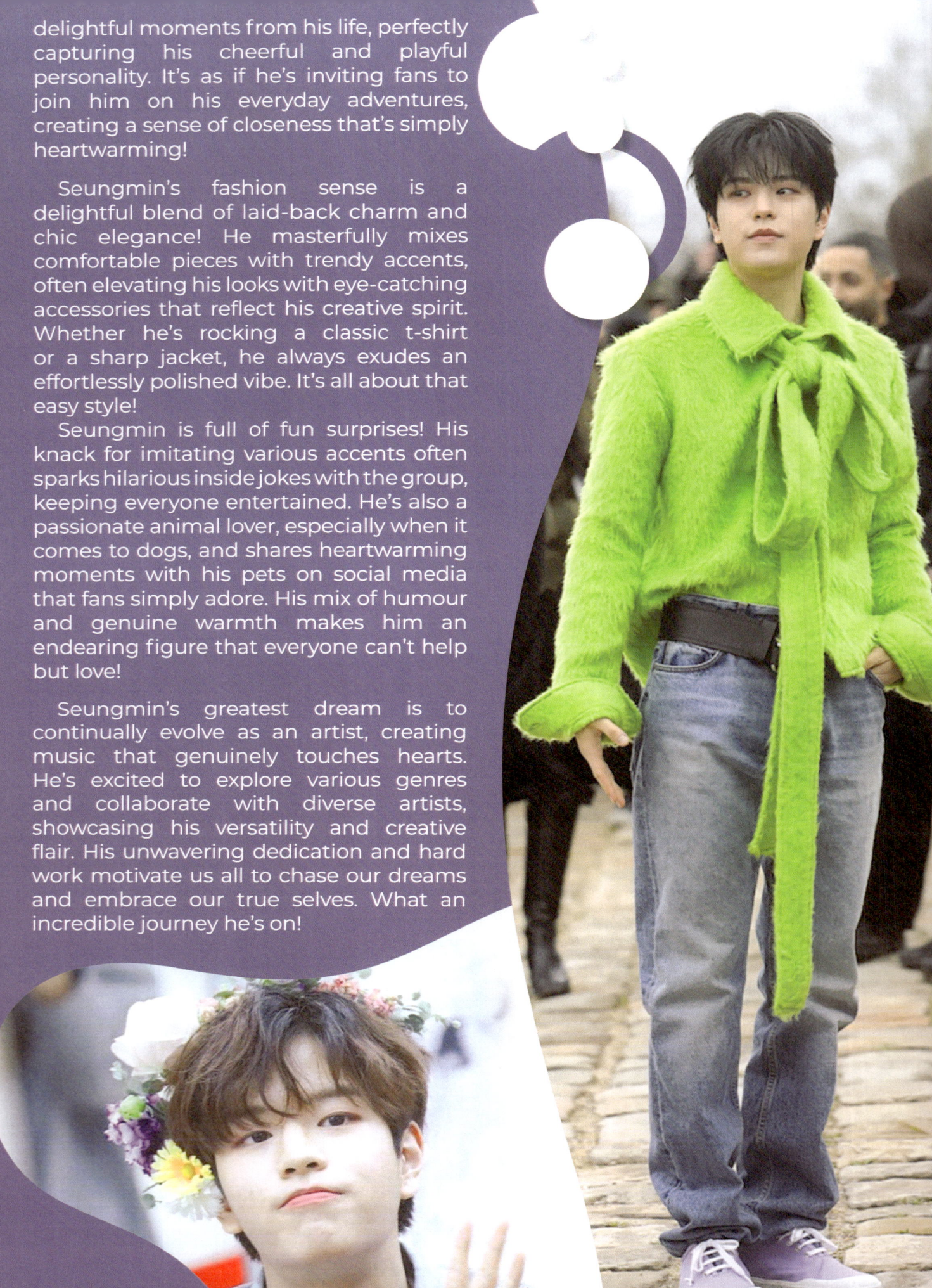

I.N

- **Real Name:** Yang Jeongin
- **Stage Name:** I.N
- **Position:** Vocalist, Maknae (youngest member)
- **Birthday:** February 8, 2001
- **Zodiac Sign:** Aquarius
- **Blood Type:** A
- **Place of Birth:** Busan, South Korea
- **Height:** 172 cm (5'8")
- **Weight:** 62 kg (137 lbs)
- **Family:** Father, mother, elder brother, younger brother
- **Favourite Colour:** Hot pink
- **Hobbies:** Singing trot, reading, watching mukbangs (food-eating videos)
- **Lucky Number:** 2
- **Fun Fact:** I.N trained as a trot singer before debuting with Stray Kids.
- **Guilty Pleasures:** Collecting plushies (he has a soft spot for cute things) and binge-watching anime series.

I.N, whose real name is Yang Jeongin, was born on 8th February 2001 in the vibrant city of Busan, South Korea. As the youngest in his family, he quickly developed a sense of resilience and independence. Before stepping into the spotlight as an idol, I.N honed his skills in traditional Korean music, particularly pansori, which laid the foundation for his incredible vocals. These early experiences ignited his passion for performance and fuelled his determination to pursue his dreams. What a remarkable journey he's had!

Known as the "Maknae on Top," I.N brings a delightful blend of confidence and playfulness to his role as the youngest member of Stray Kids! He's making strides in his English while naturally connecting with fans around the globe through his fluent Korean. I.N's passion for food is infectious, particularly his love for kalguksu (knife-cut noodles) paired with geotjeori (fresh kimchi). Fans can't help but share in his excitement as he explores new dishes with genuine joy!

In his downtime, I.N absolutely adores playing the piano, watching films, and spending quality time with his fellow members. He's a passionate animal lover, especially when it comes to his beloved pet dog, sharing countless adorable moments online. This heartfelt devotion to animals truly highlights his sweet and caring nature, making fans adore him even more! When it comes to fashion, I.N strikes the perfect balance between comfort and style, often opting for vibrant colours and playful accessories to truly express himself. How delightful!

I.N's delightful and supportive nature truly makes him the heart of the group! His vibrant energy is infectious, always lifting everyone's spirits. With an enchanting blend of innocent charm and a strong sense of responsibility, his dedication to his craft shines brightly. Fans can always rely on I.N for a warm smile or a reassuring word, making him utterly lovable!

Some fun facts about I.N? He's got a quirky obsession with rock-paper-scissors—somehow, he always wins, and it's become a funny thing among the members. Beyond that, his adorable yet determined spirit shines through when he faces challenges, leaving everyone pleasantly surprised by his persistence and success. Those playful moments and inside jokes only enhance his charm!

I.N dreams of evolving as an artist, exploring diverse music styles that ignite his creativity. His goal is to inspire others through his vibrant performances and spread positivity wherever he goes. His transformation from a young trainee to a remarkable idol is a testament to hard work and resilience, encouraging us to chase our passions and always have faith in ourselves!

DISCOGRAPHY

2020

2017
November 1
Hellevator
Single

2018
January 8
Mixtape
Album

March 26
I Am NOT
Album

August 6
I Am WHO
Album

October 22
I Am YOU
Album

2019
March 25
Clé 1: MIROH
Album

June 19
Clé 2: Yellow Wood
Album

October 8
Double Knot
Single

December 9
Clé: LEVANTER
Album

December 26
Mixtape: Gone Days
Single

2020
January 24
Step Out of Clé
Single

March 18
SKZ2020
Album

March 25
Mixtape: On Track
Single

May 20
TOP
(English version)
Single

May 26
TOP
(Japanese version)
EP

June 17
GO生 (GO LIVE)
Album

September 14
IN生 (IN LIFE)
Album

October 27
ALL IN
Album

November 26
ALL IN
(Korean Version)
Album

2021

June 26
Mixtape: Oh
Single

August 23
NOEASY
Album

November 29
Christmas EveL
EP

December 23
SKZ2021
Album

2022

March 18
ODDINARY
Album

June 22
CIRCUS
Japanese EP

October 7
MAXIDENT
Album

December 21
SKZ-REPLAY
Album

2023

February 22
THE SOUND
Japanese Album

June 2
5-STAR
Album

September 6
Social Path / Super Bowl
(Japanese Version)
Japanese EP

November 10
ROCK-STAR
Album

2024

May 10
Lose My Breath
(Feat. Charlie Puth)
Single

May 13
Lose My Breath
(Remixes)
Single

July 19
ATE
Album

July 22
Chk Chk Boom
(Remixes)
Album

July 23
SLASH
(From "Deadpool & Wolverine")
Single

October 7
NIGHT
(Korean Version)
Single

NIGHT
(English Version)
Single

NIGHT
Single

Falling Up
(English Version)
Single

Falling Up
Single

November 13
GIANT
Album

ALBUM COVERS

2017 — 2018

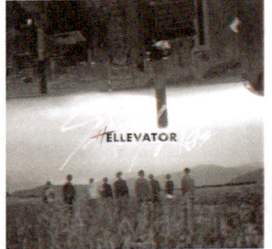   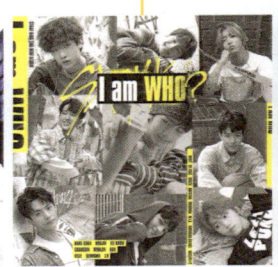 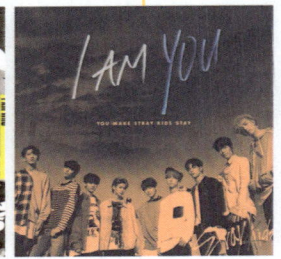

2019

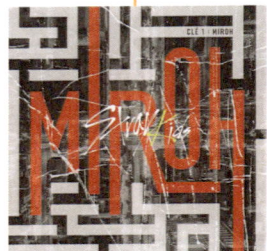   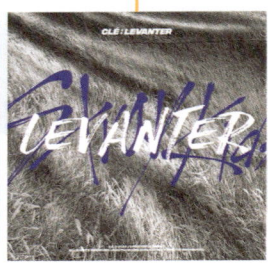 

2020

2020

2021

2022

2023 — 2024

2024

2024
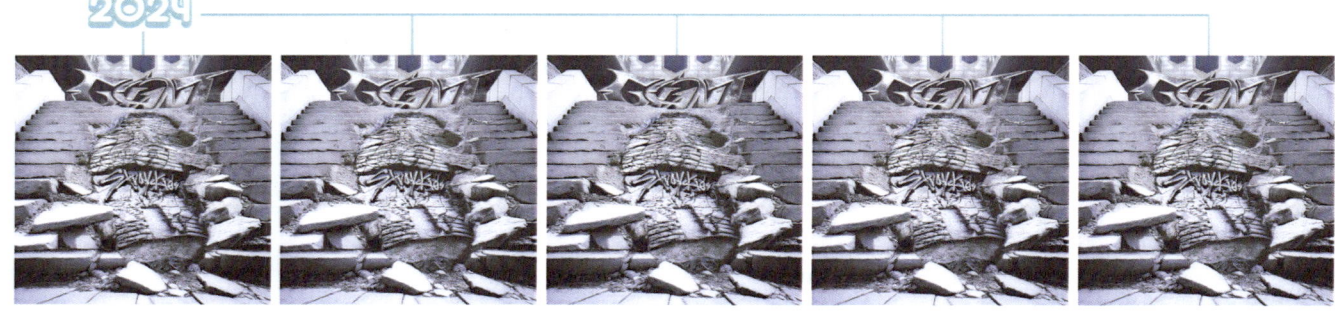

UNFORGETTABLE CONCERTS: THE ENERGY OF STRAY KIDS

Stray Kids are absolutely more than just a K-pop group—they're a phenomenal experience that sweeps you off your feet! Their concerts are nothing short of electric, creating an atmosphere that buzzes with energy long after the final note has played. Fans can expect each performance to be a vibrant celebration, where every song is infused with passion and excitement.

From their debut world tour, "District 9: Unlock," to the thrilling "Maniac" tour, each event showcases the incredible chemistry they share with STAYs around the globe. It's as if they transcend conventional concerts, inviting everyone into a joyous community that dances and sings together as one. Their charismatic presence and powerful performances leave a lasting impression, making each show a cherished memory for all who attend.

So, if you're lucky enough to catch them live, get ready for an unforgettable ride! Prepare to be swept away by the music and the overwhelming sense of connection that comes from being part of the Stray Kids family. You won't just be a spectator; you'll feel like an essential part of something extraordinary!

District 9: Unlock Tour

Kicking off their adventure with the "District 9: Unlock" tour in 2019 and 2020, Stray Kids truly took the world by storm, captivating fans with their electrifying performances! This milestone marked their very first world tour, celebrating the launch of their debut studio album, GO生 (GO LIVE). The atmosphere at each concert was simply electric! Every show radiated its own unique energy, but one thing was perfectly clear: the thrill and joy shared between the members and their devoted fans was palpable.

The theme of "unlocking" new experiences resonated deeply, beautifully mirroring Stray Kids' artistic growth and the journey they embarked on together. It was more than just a tour; it was a heartfelt celebration of their progress and connection with fans around the globe. Each performance felt like a shared adventure, filled with laughter, passion, and an overwhelming sense of community.

Some unforgettable highlights included stunning choreography, heartfelt moments of interaction, and soaring vocals that left everyone in awe. Fans were treated to magnificent stages that only added to the excitement! The tour wasn't just about the music; it was about forging memorable bonds and creating lasting memories that fans will cherish forever. Stray Kids truly unlocked a world of joy and inspiration, leaving an indelible mark on the hearts of all who experienced it!

Here are some of the highlights:

Heartfelt Fan Interactions: The band truly cherished their connection with fans, expressing genuine gratitude that made everyone feel included in something extraordinary. Bang Chan consistently took the time to engage with the audience, ensuring each show felt personal and intimate. It was a delightful experience for all!

Visually Stunning Performances: The stage design was truly extraordinary! With breathtaking visuals and dazzling lighting, the atmosphere perfectly complemented energetic tracks like "God's Menu" and "Back Door." Fans couldn't resist joining in, creating an unforgettable vibe!

Emotional Moments: Songs like "Yours" and "Hellevator" truly tugged at the heartstrings, allowing fans to forge a deeper connection with the members. The raw emotion of these performances sparked cheers and applause, beautifully highlighting the incredible bond between the group and their devoted fans!

Maniac World Tour

After the remarkable triumph of their debut tour, Stray Kids launched into the "Maniac" world tour in 2022, taking their electrifying performances to astonishing new heights! This exciting journey celebrated their album *NOEASY* and covered a whirlwind of locations across Asia, North America, and Europe. The "Maniac" tour was truly a tribute to self-confidence and resilience, and the title track "MANIAC" encapsulated that bold spirit flawlessly.

The atmosphere in the arenas was nothing short of electric, with fans igniting the space with their energy, cheering and dancing along to every beat. You could feel the pulse of excitement in the air! It was a beautiful sight to see thousands of fans united by their love for Stray Kids, creating a vibrant and unforgettable experience.

Among the many standout moments, fans were treated to dazzling performances, surprise stages, and heartwarming interactions that truly made the tour special. Whether it was the unforgettable choreography or the passionate fan chants, each performance was a celebration of the unique bond between the group and their loyal supporters. All in all, the "Maniac" tour was a joyous occasion, leaving everyone exhilarated and eager for what's to come next!

Here are some of the highlights:

Breathtaking Visuals: The staging was absolutely spectacular! With innovative choreography and stylish outfits that perfectly showcased each member's unique flair, it was a feast for the eyes. The visuals had fans buzzing with excitement!

Special Stages: Stray Kids truly impressed fans with their individual talents during special stages! From Hyunjin's breathtaking dance solos to Felix's enchanting performances, each member brought their own unique flair, shining brightly and winning over hearts everywhere. What an amazing display of talent!

Surprise Guest Appearances: Picture the thrill when Stray Kids delighted fans with surprise collaborations and guest performances at their concerts! Those unforgettable moments added an extra spark, making each show truly special. What a joy it is to witness such excitement live!

A Lasting Connection

Stray Kids truly shine in their tours, effortlessly connecting with fans in such a meaningful way. Their genuine gratitude, electrifying performances, and heartfelt messages remind us that we're all part of this incredible journey together. Each concert is more than just a show; it's a lively celebration of our shared memories and experiences. Stray Kids' concerts radiate unity, passion, and the amazing bond with STAYs, leaving us feeling inspired and ready to take on the world! What an unforgettable experience!

SONG MEANINGS AND THEMES

Stray Kids have an incredible talent for capturing our emotions and experiences through their music! Their lyrics resonate with themes of self-expression, resilience, and the exhilarating journey of growing up. We've all navigated the ups and downs of fitting in and discovering our true selves, and Stray Kids remind us beautifully that it's absolutely wonderful to celebrate our individuality.

With their powerful sound and relatable messages, they create a welcoming space where we feel both understood and inspired. Listening to their songs is like having a warm-hearted chat with a friend who just gets it! They challenge us to embrace our uniqueness and believe that we can overcome any obstacle that comes our way.

It's truly uplifting to see how Stray Kids connect with us on such a personal level. Their music isn't just a song; it's a source of encouragement that makes us feel like we're part of something bigger. So, let's keep celebrating our journeys together with the infectious energy that their music brings!

God's Menu: A Taste of Individuality

Absolutely "God's Menu" is truly a gem that resonates with so many of us. It's a magnificent anthem that invites everyone to step away from the ordinary and embrace the extraordinary aspects of who we are. Through its clever metaphor of a menu, the song beautifully illustrates how each person contributes their own unique flavours and talents, making the world a much richer place.

With its infectious beat and vibrant energy, "God's Menu" not only gets you moving but also inspires you to celebrate your individuality! It's all about standing tall and owning your uniqueness, which feels particularly empowering during those formative years. You can't help but feel a rush of self-confidence as you immerse yourself in its upbeat rhythm.

And hey, we know you're itching to dive deeper—where are the lyrics, right? No worries at all; they're just below. So go ahead, sing along, and let your true colours shine! Embrace this thrilling journey of self-discovery; you've got this! ^-^

VERSE 1

우리의메뉴를만들고
We create our own menu

모두의입맛에맞춰
Tailoring it to everyone's taste

다채워넣어
Filling it up completely

어둠속에숨은모습들
Hidden figures in the dark

내가던진이스파이스를
Taste this spice I throw

다먹어봐, 미식가가돼봐
Try it all, become a gourmet

CHORUS

이제부터가시작이야
This is just the beginning

여기서뭘선택할지
What will we choose here?

선택은우리, 모두다가짜
The choice is ours, all fake

이젠완전히달라져
Now we've completely changed

단한번의기회를가져
Let's take this one chance

VERSE 2

위험한맛의향연
A feast of dangerous flavors

지금우리가요리해
Now we cook

자극적인맛으로가득한
Full of stimulating tastes

이건우리의메뉴, 맛보여줄게
This is our menu, let me show you

CHORUS

이제부터가시작이야
This is just the beginning

여기서뭘선택할지
What will we choose here?

선택은우리, 모두다가짜
The choice is ours, all fake

이젠완전히달라져
Now we've completely changed

단한번의기회를가져
Let's take this one chance

BRIDGE

기다려왔던이순간
The moment we've been waiting for

이제우리가요리해
Now we cook

어두운맛을밝히고
Bringing light to dark flavors

하늘에닿게될거야
We will reach the sky

CHORUS

이제부터가시작이야
This is just the beginning

여기서뭘선택할지
What will we choose here?

선택은우리, 모두다가짜
The choice is ours, all fake

이젠완전히달라져
Now we've completely changed

단한번의기회를가져
Let's take this one chance

Stray Kids' Coolest Collabs with Movies, Anime, and Games!

Stray Kids are not just renowned for their electrifying songs and breathtaking live performances—they've also partnered with some incredibly cool shows, anime, and even video games! If you're a fan of movies, anime, or gaming, it's highly likely that you've encountered a Stray Kids track without even realising it. Their infectious energy and catchy melodies have a way of sneaking into the background, adding a little extra magic to whatever you're watching or playing.

One of the things that truly sets Stray Kids apart is their collaborative spirit. They've scored the soundtracks for popular anime like "Tower of God" and teamed up with beloved franchises to create music that resonates with fans on multiple levels. Their ability to blend their distinct sound with these diverse mediums brings a fresh and exciting twist that we all adore. It just goes to show how versatile they are—whether they're pumping up an epic battle scene or providing the perfect backdrop for a heartfelt moment, their music enhances the experience in ways that often leave us wanting more.

So, whether you're vibing to their latest release or discovering a hidden gem in an anime episode, Stray Kids' tracks are sure to make a lasting impression. Their collaborations have not only elevated their music but also deepened our appreciation for the art forms they intersect with, making each listen all the more special. Here's to celebrating the incredible synergy between Stray Kids and the world of entertainment—there are just so many reasons to love them!

"TOP" for Tower of God (Anime)

Have you ever watched an anime with a theme song so perfect it gave you chills? That's exactly what Stray Kids delivered with "TOP" for the hit anime Tower of God (Kami no Tou) in 2020. It's not just any anime—it's based on a super popular webtoon, so the stakes were high. Stray Kids didn't just sing in one language either—they recorded the song in Korean, Japanese, and English! "TOP" totally captures that feeling of never giving up, which ties in perfectly with the anime's adventurous and mysterious vibe. If you haven't checked it out yet, grab some popcorn and dive in. You might just find your new favorite anime and Stray Kids song!

"Hello Stranger" for Pop Out Boy! (K-Drama

Ever dreamed of your favorite comic book character coming to life? That's the wild plot of the K-drama Pop Out Boy! (만찢남녀), and guess what? Stray Kids gave us the super catchy track "Hello Stranger" to go along with it. It's upbeat, playful, and fits perfectly with the drama's fun and quirky vibe. If you're looking for something lighthearted to binge-watch, this is a great pick. And of course, Stray Kids' music will make it all the more fun!

"SLASH" for League of Legends (Game Collab)

If you're a gamer (or even just someone who loves to win), you've probably heard of League of Legends. In 2022, Stray Kids got involved in this major gaming world with their track "SLASH" for the League of Legends World Championship. This song is fierce—it's all about going full power and taking on the competition, which matches the intensity of the game perfectly. If you're a League fan, this one's a must-listen. Even if you don't game, "SLASH" is such a banger that you'll feel like you're ready to take on anything.

"Thunderous" Remix for Arcane (Netflix Series)

Okay, so Arcane is basically League of Legends brought to life in one of the coolest ways possible. The Netflix series took off in 2021, and Stray Kids jumped in with a special remix of their song "Thunderous" for the promo. The remix was just as fiery as the original, perfectly matching the series' intense and rebellious vibes. It wasn't part of the soundtrack, but it made the Arcane hype even more real! If you love powerful visuals and even more powerful music, check out Arcane and crank up that remix.

"Scars" for Re: Revenge - Yokubo no Hate ni (Japanese Drama)

Stray Kids hit us in the feels with their track "Scars" for the Japanese drama Re: Revenge - Yokubo no Hate ni in 2021. The drama is all about revenge and overcoming pain, and "Scars" fits it perfectly with lyrics about healing and finding strength after being hurt. If you're into dramas that hit deep, this one's for you—and Stray Kids' emotional song will take you on the same rollercoaster of emotions as the characters.

Individual Projects of the Members

Stray Kids truly shines with their incredibly talented lineup! Each member brings something unique to the table, showcasing their diverse skills through various solo projects that perfectly reflect their individual passions. It's such a joy to see them express themselves creatively in different ways, isn't it?

From mesmerizing vocal performances to electrifying dance routines, the members don't just stick to the group dynamic; they step out and truly shine on their own. Whether it's producing their own music, exploring acting, or dabbling in artistic collaborations, each solo venture is a testament to their hard work and dedication. It definitely inspires fans to embrace their own dreams and pursuits!

Let's celebrate these exciting individual journeys! They remind us that while teamwork is crucial, there's immense value in recognising and nurturing our own unique talents. So, here's to Stray Kids—may their inspiring individual pursuits motivate us all to chase after what we love!

Bang Chan

Mixtapes: Bang Chan has blessed us with some incredible solo tracks and mixtapes, like "Chan's Room," where he truly pours his heart into his music. His lyrics resonate with so many of us, often drawing from personal experiences, making it feel like we're right there beside him!

Production Work: As the leader of Stray Kids, Bang Chan plays a pivotal role in producing our favourite tracks. His talent for blending different genres adds to that unique sound we all adore. It's no wonder he's such a key part of their success!

Lee Know

Dance Projects: Lee Know's dance skills are absolutely phenomenal! He frequently shares his solo dance performances online, showcasing his incredible creativity and passion. It's always a delight to watch him dance!

Variety Show Appearances: He's a regular on various variety shows, where his charming personality and sense of humour truly shine. It's impossible not to love how relatable and entertaining he is!

Changbin

Solo Mixtapes: Changbin has gifted us with his incredible mixtapes, like *Black Hole*, where he boldly explores his thoughts and emotions. His rap skills are absolutely phenomenal, and he's unafraid to share his struggles, which truly inspires us to persevere through tough times!

Collaboration: On top of that, he plays a pivotal role in writing and producing music for Stray Kids, infusing our favourite tracks with his unique flair. How amazing is that?

Hyunjin

Artistic Projects: Hyunjin is not only an incredible performer but also a gifted artist! He delights his fans by sharing his stunning drawings and artwork, giving us a lovely peek into his creative world.

Acting Roles: He's tried his hand at acting as well, showcasing his undeniable charisma and charm on screen—something fans absolutely adore!

Han

Solo Releases: Han has released some fantastic solo tracks that highlight his amazing vocals and rap skills. His music beautifully captures his journey and strikes a chord with fans who relate to his experiences.

Songwriting: Not only that, but he's also an incredibly talented songwriter! His contributions to many of Stray Kids' songs add depth and meaning, making them truly special.

Felix

Vocal Covers: Felix has dazzled us with his incredible vocal covers on social media! His rich, deep voice never fails to leave us in awe. It's such a fantastic way for him to connect with fans and showcase his talent!

Fashion Projects: He's also making waves in the fashion world, joining exciting collaborations that truly reflect his stylish flair. Felix is definitely a trendsetter among us!

I.N

Solo Songs: I.N has delighted fans with his solo tracks that truly showcase his sweet vocals! His music beautifully captures youthful emotions, making it so easy for us to connect with him.

Participation in Writing: What's even more impressive is his involvement in writing lyrics for Stray Kids. This not only highlights his growth as an artist but also his incredible creativity!

Seungmin

Vocal Focus: We simply adore Seungmin's powerful voice! His covers of popular songs showcase his incredible range, and they're always a hit with fans!

Songwriting Contributions: Seungmin has also shared his lyrical talent in Stray Kids' songs, bringing his unique perspective and relatable themes, making the music feel even more personal. It's all so wonderful!

Stray Kids

Inspiration for Us

The individual projects of Stray Kids members inspire us to dive into our passions and interests wholeheartedly! They demonstrate that being part of a group doesn't mean we can't shine individually. Their journeys encourage us to pursue our dreams—whether in music, art, or any creative endeavour. Each project celebrates the power of self-expression and personal growth, reminding us that we can forge our own paths while being uplifted by a supportive community. How wonderful is that!

Inspirational Messages from Stray Kids

Stray Kids are not only exceptional performers; they're also brimming with wisdom and positivity! Their uplifting words remind us to chase our dreams with passion, face challenges head-on, and wholeheartedly embrace our authentic selves. Each member's unique perspective adds a beautiful layer to their message, creating a vibrant tapestry of encouragement that truly resonates.

It's a joy to explore this delightful collection of inspiring quotes from each member! They remind us that we're all on this journey together, reinforcing the idea that no one needs to face their struggles alone. Whether it's pushing through obstacles or celebrating our achievements, their messages are like little sparks of joy that ignite our motivation.

So, let's dive in and soak up that inspiration! Stray Kids' enthusiasm is contagious, and their words have the power to uplift and energise us. Together, let's celebrate our dreams and support one another as we navigate this adventure called life!

Bang Chan on Overcoming Challenges:

> *Every challenge
> we face is a step toward our dreams.
> If we give up,
> we'll never know how far we could have gone.*

Felix on Overcoming Fear:

> *Don't let fear hold you back.
> It's normal to feel scared,
> but pushing through that
> fear can lead to amazing things.*

I.N on Dreams:

> *Chase your dreams with
> all your heart.
> Even if it gets tough,
> don't forget why you started.*

Seungmin on Hard Work:

> *Hard work beats talent when
> talent doesn't work hard.*

Hyunjin on Resilience:

> *It's okay to stumble and fall.
> What matters is that
> you get back up and keep going.*

Changbin on Pursuing Passions:

> *Follow what you love and
> don't let anyone tell you it's not possible.
> If you believe in yourself,
> you can achieve anything.*

Han on Embracing Uniqueness:

> *Don't be afraid to show who you are.
> Every flaw makes you unique,
> and that's what makes you beautiful.*

Bang Chan on Setting Goals:

> *If you have a dream,
> write it down and take small steps every day.
> Progress is progress,
> no matter how small.*

Seungmin on Positivity:

> *A positive mindset can change your life.
> Focus on the good,
> and you'll see the world in a brighter way.*

I.N on Self-Discovery:

> *Life is a journey of discovering who you are.
> Take your time and enjoy every moment.*

Stray Kids' messages truly inspire us to dream boldly and face challenges head-on! Their words remind us that we're not alone in our journeys; we're all in this together, cheering each other on. It's so uplifting to know that self-belief is the essential first step to turning our dreams into reality!

Let's take these empowering words to heart and embrace the adventures that lie ahead! Every challenge we encounter is an opportunity to grow, and with the encouragement from Stray Kids, we can tackle anything that comes our way.

So, let's keep their spirit alive as we set out on our own unique paths. Remember, with courage and belief in ourselves, there's no limit to what we can achieve!

Stray Kids

www.ingramcontent.com/pod-product-compliance
Lightning Source LLC
Chambersburg PA
CBRC100224100526
44590CB00009B/151